Evaporation

William B. Rice

Consultant

Scot Oschman, Ph.D.

Palos Verdes Peninsula Unified School District

Rancho Palos Verdes, California

Publishing Credits

Dona Herweck Rice, *Editor-in-Chief*; Lee Aucoin, *Creative Director*; Don Tran, *Print Production Manager;* Timothy J. Bradley, *Illustration Manager*; Chris McIntyre, *Editorial Director*; James Anderson, *Associate Editor*; Jamey Acosta, *Associate Editor*; Jane Gould, *Editor*; Peter Balaskas, *Editorial Administrator*; Neri Garcia, *Senior Designer*; Stephanie Reid, *Photo Editor*; Rachelle Cracchiolo, M.S.Ed., *Publisher*

Image Credits

cover Roman Sigaev/Shutterstock; p.1 Roman Sigaev/Shutterstock; p. 4 Fabrizio Argonauta/Dreamstime; p.5 (top) A_Sh/Shutterstock, (bottom) vblinov/Shutterstock; p.6 Peter Clark/Shutterstock; p.7 Pavel K/Shutterstock; p.8 Nikolay Okhitin/Shutterstock; p.9 Stephanie Reid; p.10 ArtyFree/Shutterstock; p.11 Bernd Meiseberg/Shutterstock; p.12 Mark Lorch/Shutterstock; p.13 (top) Vidux/Shutterstock, (bottom) PeterG/Shutterstock; p.14 Nico Smit/iStockphoto; p.15 Hemera Technologies/Gettty Images; p.16 Jacek Chabraszewski/Shutterstock; p.17 Alexandr Ozernov/iStockphoto; p.18 Peter Wollinga/Shutterstock; p.19 (left) Ramona Heim/Shutterstock, (right) Dmitriy Bryndin/Shutterstock; p. 20 Hemera Technologies/Getty Images; p.21 (top) Jim Lopes/Shutterstock, (bottom) stock master/Shutterstock; p.22 Lars Christensen/Shutterstock; p.23 (top) Stephanie Reid, (bottom) SebStock/Shutterstock; p.24 Dudarev Mikhail/Shutterstock; p.25 (top) Kesu/Shutterstock, (bottom) Jozsef Szasz-Fabian/Shutterstock; p.26 jovannig/Shutterstock; p.27 (top) Raimundas/Shutterstock, (bottom left) Rudy Lopez Photography/Shutterstock, (bottom right) Nobor/Shutterstock; p.28 Rocket400 Studio/Shutterstock; p.29 Ana Clark; p.32 (left) Roberto Danovaro, (right) Roberto Danovaro

Teacher Created Materials
5301 Oceanus Drive
Huntington Beach, CA 92649-1030
http://www.tcmpub.com

ISBN 978-1-4333-1417-9

Printed by: 590835
Printed in: China

Table of Contents

Where Does It Go?

It rains all night long. Then the rain stops. Everything is wet. The sun comes out. The water goes away. It seems like magic! Where does it go?

It is not magic. It is **evaporation** (i-vap-uh-RAY-shun). The water evaporates. It changes from a liquid to a gas.

Rain makes things wet.

The sun helps dry the rain.

Evaporation

Evaporation happens when a liquid becomes a gas. Water is a liquid. Air is made of gases. The water changes its form. It becomes part of the air.

Condensation (kohn-den-SEY-shun) happens when a gas becomes a liquid.

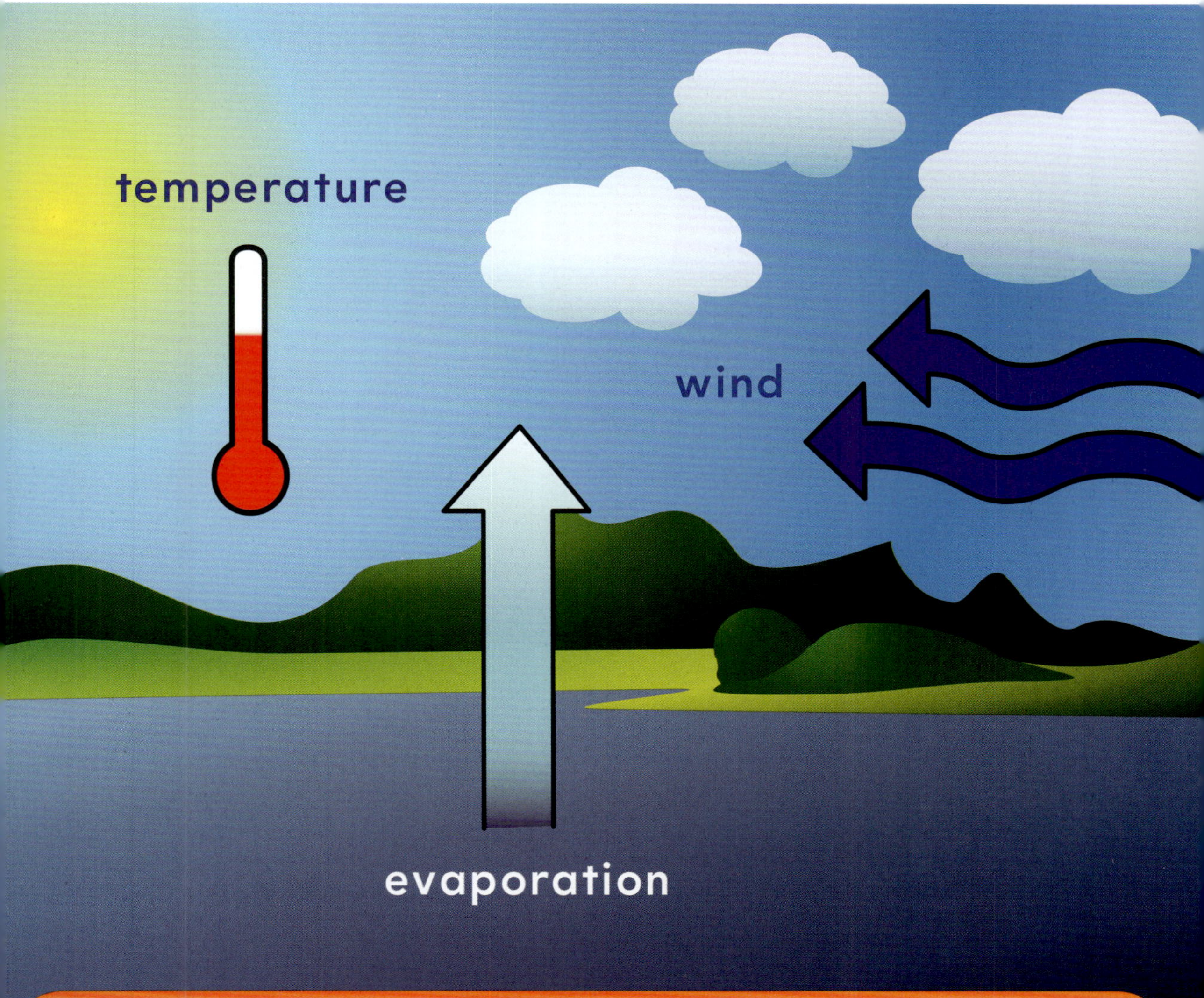

Wind and high temperatures make water evaporate faster.

A liquid is made of tiny parts. The parts are called **molecules** (MOL-uh-kyoolz). You cannot see them. They may escape from the liquid. That is when evaporation happens.

This is a large model of a water molecule. A single water molecule is too small to see.

The molecules in a liquid move around. They move fast when they get hot. They bump into each other. The molecules on top might get bumped off! They turn into a gas.

Think about popcorn popping. When popcorn gets hot, some of it gets bumped out of the pan. This can help you understand evaporation.

evaporation

Liquid that gets very hot evaporates fast. Cold liquid evaporates slowly.

Desert heat evaporates water quickly. Animals who live there must drink whenever they find water.

Fun Fact

If a liquid gets so cold that it freezes, then it becomes a solid.

Liquid that evaporates becomes a gas. We can always see the liquid. Sometimes we cannot see the gas.

Air is filled with gases. Can you see them?

Sometimes it is hot, but evaporation is slow. That is because the air is already full. There is not much room for more gas. That is called **saturation** (sach-uh-REY-shun). There is no room for more molecules.

In the rainforest, sometimes things stay wet because the air is already very wet.

Wind also helps liquid evaporate. Big wind means fast evaporation!

Wind helps these things dry fast.

Fun Fact

Did you ever shake your hands to dry them? It works because of evaporation!

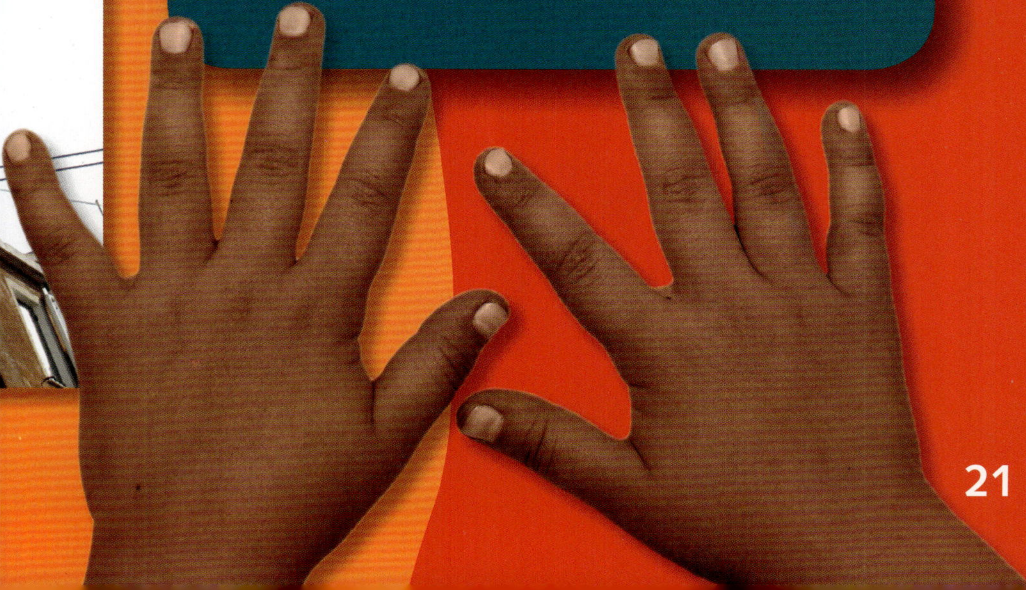

The Water Cycle

Evaporation is part of the **water cycle**. The water cycle is how water changes. It changes its form. The water cycle is important to life on Earth.

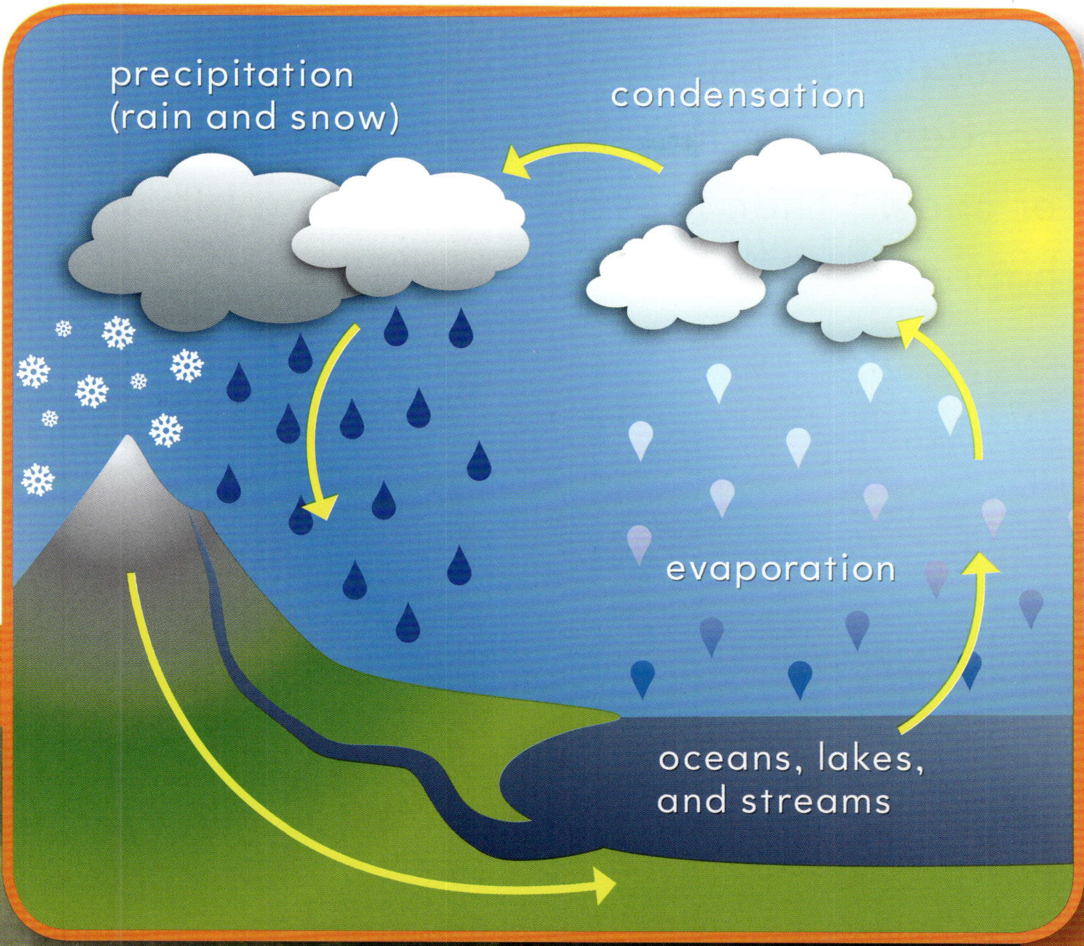
precipitation
(rain and snow)
condensation
evaporation
oceans, lakes,
and streams

Water on Earth evaporates. Then it condenses. It may fall to Earth as rain or snow. Then it evaporates again. This happens again and again.

All liquid does not evaporate at the same rate. Water evaporates fast. Milk or oil may evaporate more slowly.

Evaporation is just one part of the cycle. But the cycle would not work without it!

Science Lab: What Is Evaporation?

You can see evaporation in action if you follow these steps.

Materials:

- 2 clear plastic cups
- marker
- plastic wrap
- water
- a sunny day

Procedure:

1. Fill each cup with water. Be sure the cups have the same amount of water.
2. Put plastic wrap tightly over one cup.
3. Mark the water line on both cups.
4. Place the cups outside in the sun where nothing will knock them over.

5. Check the cups after two hours. Did the water go down in either cup? Mark the new water line.

6. Check again in two more hours. Mark the water line again.

7. Keep checking over time. You will see that the cup that is not covered is losing its water. But the water did not spill. It evaporated in the heat of the sun. The plastic covering does not allow the water from the second cup to evaporate, so it should all still be there.

Glossary

condensation—the act of changing a gas to a liquid

evaporation—the act of changing a liquid to a gas

molecules—very tiny parts that make up solids, liquids, and gases

saturation—when something is filled up

water cycle—the process that water goes through as it changes from one state to another

Index

A Scientist Today

Roberto Danovaro lives in Italy. He is a scientist who studies sea animals. He found the first multi-cell animal we know that lives without oxygen! It lives in the mud on the ocean floor.

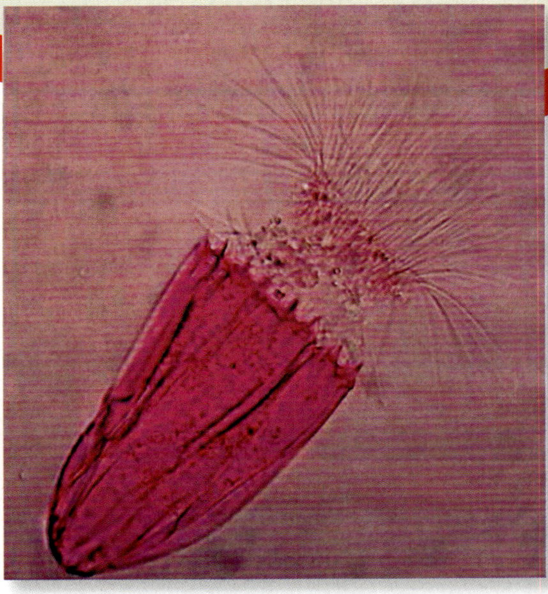